In the Blue of Time

JOAN TABER

For my family

CONTENTS

A special thank you to my friends Dana Cochran and Helen Campbell for their ongoing support and encouragement. Thank you, too, David Jackier, Polly Purvis, Harry Greenberg, Nora Beeman, and Judith Taber for cheering me on; and Giuseppe Battista for having introduced me to Salvatore Quasimodo *ed è subito sera.*

if it doesn't come bursting out of you
in spite of everything,
don't do it.
Charles Bukowski

Vigil

In the silence after dying,
the voices of our children
float across the sea divide
between time and nowhere else;
and we must learn to listen
to the greening of the leaves,
to the rustle of the silken page;
and we must learn the language
of the sinking cirrus cloud,
its softly rounded vowels
that paint the bluing sky
as mourning becomes our years
and then our turn to die.

The Day Logan Ran Through the Museum

Dear Logan, remember what you felt today
as you ran from window to window,
from exhibit to exhibit, calling for bears
and caribous and foxes to come and play with you;
remember the thrill of too much to take in,
the wonder of letters that form word after word;
remember the crashing sounds of sea
in the room where the blue whale no longer swims free.
Remember the grownups slowing you down.
Don't listen to us when we slow you down!
And don't listen to yourself when you grow up
and try to slow down because you think you should.
Don't get discouraged because there's so much to learn,
because no one can learn it all, and that's hard to learn.
Remember the joy of newness you felt,
your fresh way of looking at the old blue world,
the majesty of muskox and spotted leopard,
the sadness of felled trees, the disappearing elephants,
the eyes of the stuffed bear telling you his story.
Remember this day when life swivels and flips,
when impossible is the only word you hear;
remember what you felt as you ran today
from exhibit to exhibit at the museum in the city,
because that's what living is, or should be;
that's the magic of breathing daily.
Don't let it spurt into stardust and drift;
don't let it escape to the moon. It's yours to keep
forever—the day you ran through the museum.

To the Homeless Man Beaten In the Park

It wasn't so much the beating you took—
it was the gentle way you picked up your cap
from the ground and pulled it over your unwashed hair;
it was the way you squared your thin spine and shoulders
under the torn and freshly bloodied shirt,
your eyes scanning hues of fallen leaves,
their particular shades of orange and brown,
as though your tormentors were no longer there,
no longer pounding you down,
as though everything were as it ever had been,
and you still king of the mountain top

that reminded me of my father and the beating he took
in his hospital gown,
the gentle way he must have straightened the sheet,
pulling it over his bruises and blood,
the way he smiled through panes of the hospital window
and talked to the building across the way,
asking it questions like, "What do you think about all day?"
as though his tormentors were no longer there
no longer pounding him down,
as though everything were as it ever had been,
and he still king of the mountain top.

5

Horses & Other Animals Like Me

Come to me
as far as the fence.
I'll feed you
apples and hay.
Let's pretend
this rain has gone
behind the sun
you bring to me today;
let's pretend to make
sense of the way
you were corralled
and I set free
as though God noticed
some difference
between you and me.

Wishing the Dead

There was a time I used to wish
my father would be dead; but no one knew,
because my words were camouflaged
as explosions in my head
that pounded the tender childhood threads
connecting right and left of brain,
creating a percussion, string-like sound
that no one ever heard.
I wanted him to lie quite still
in a stardust silk-lined coffin
—mahogany and filigreed, polished
like the night. I wanted him
to wear a suit, and on his lips a smile,
and in his eyes, a certain softness
beneath his lids sewn safely shut;
then friends and family would gather round
and weep for such a loss.
And when I pictured him like that
it was too easy to will him back.

Winters In Morning
(for my brother)

When winter dragged across the skyline
the harbor froze and fish eyed under glass
at the tip of the thin-lipped firth.

Rutted roads growled under its ice load,
and buildings tumbled into fog each night
at the edge of the pock-round dip.

We carved out caves and called them igloos
and brought in bears and sheep and lions
from the belly of the round-eyed earth.

Spinning tops and cast-iron armies
guarded our secrets from grown-up sneers
on the cupid bowline of their dream-dead lips.

Our war dance flickered like film on shadow
melting into dream time and raw-red hearts
on the crest of the whale-winter surf.

Canopies capped icicle dreamscapes
crashing though the diamond-tip ridge
at the snap of the cutting wind whip,
and winter slipped daily into our mornings.

Rob Purvis

May you rest in peace in your urn of ashes—
or if souls wander somewhere beyond our ken,
may you wander in fields of calm and carnations,
may you wander through Handel and constellations.
Your years on earth weren't kind or fair,
but in the whirling mix of frenzy and patience
you learned how to glean rather than despair.
May you rest in peace in your urn of ashes—
or if souls float away over somewhere's horizon
may you float in shades of gold leaf and silver,
may you float on enchanted carpets of blue.
Your years on earth were sometimes shattered
beyond or within your control is no matter.
May you rest in peace in your urn of ashes—
or if souls get to return and try life again,
may you return as prince of all the mountains,
may you return in springtime on a ray of sun.

The Bests

The best thank-you note I ever received
was from Kyla when she was seven:
It read, "Dear Mommy,
thank you for cleaning up my vomit."

The best haircut I ever had
was the handiwork of my mother.
I was five, and my bangs
reminded me of steps.

The best friend I ever had was
my dog Rebel. He kissed my face
when I cried and took care of me
until he got sick and died.

The best grownup I ever knew was
George. He made us laugh
and spoke gently to us. His voice
sang something like honey.

The best plan I ever made was
with Polly. We were going to ride
across the High Plains of Wyoming
on wild palominos.

The best brother I ever had was
Tony when he was eight.
He was kind then, frail and thin, so
I fought his battles for him.

The best funeral I ever attended was
for a baby sparrow. It had twisted its neck
and lay like a speck in the yard.
I dug a hole to bury it.

The best surprise I ever had was
from a baby sparrow. I thought it had died,
so I dug a hole to bury it,
but it flapped its wings and managed to fly.

The best book I ever read was
Pride and Prejudice. I was hoping
Elizabeth would marry Mr. Darcy
in the end, and she did.

The best greeting I ever received was
from Jogi. He picked me up
and swung me all around. I had
never seen him before.

The best talk I ever had was
with Bärbel. She was honest
and swung me all around. I had
never heard such honesty before.

The best hot chocolate I ever drank was
at the train station in Florence.
It was a year of heartbreak
and I had been shivering.

The best morning I ever woke to was
on the island of Korčula.
I had slept outside and there was dew in my eyes.
I had never felt such dew before.

The best idea I ever had was
to write this a list of bests. It made me
smile and put things away.

Divorce

No way to divide the sofa
so you took the base
to your furnished room,
and I took the cushions
to my new little place.
No way to divide
a reel-to-reel
so you took the recorder
and I took the tapes,
and you had the base
so I took the cushions
to my new little place,
and you took the base
to your furnished room;
but you had the recorder
and I had the tapes,
so the music stayed
between Earth
and the moon.
No way to divide the living
room, so we gave the house
to our hungry lawyers,
and you took a dollar
to your furnished room,
and I took a dime
from your employers
and spent it on paint
for my new little place;
and you had the recorder
but I had the tapes,
so the music played
in two little tombs.
No way to divide
our memories,
so you took the bad ones
and I did, too,
and the good ones stayed
between sunset and noon.
But you had a dollar
and I did, too,

and I had cushions
for my new little place,
and you put the recorder
in the deepest corner
of your furnished room.
No way to divide the children,
so you took weekends
and I took weekdays,
and you took a dollar
to your furnished room;
and you had the base
and the recorder, too,
and I took the tapes
to my new little place
with cushions and paint
and a dollar
without a face.
No way to divide
a nucleus
so we left it behind
with the music
to chime.
No way to divide
a season in song
so we stashed
it under
music and gloom.
But you took the base
and I had a dollar,
and we wove new lives
on the broken loom.

For Sprinky, Ziggy, & All the Forgotten

Little cat, will you go to Heaven
where you'll want for nothing and never feel pain?
We have to know this will be true for you
as it's true for all the animals of the world—
pigs to slaughter, carriage horses gasping,
dogs disappearing in alleys and deserts,
cows discarded when their milk runs dry.
We have to know this is true for us, too—
that you'll wait for us and greet us when we die.

Little dog, have you gone to Heaven
where you're watching over the ones who loved you?
We have to know this is true for you
as it's true for all the children of the world—
tiny babies who die in utero, toddlers killed in war,
teenagers who die for a night of partying,
the ones who jump in front of trains
or slump with the needle still in their vein,
We have to know this is true for us, too—
that you'll wait for us and greet us when we die.

Little prayer, will you go to Heaven,
where kindness rules and old age is veneration?
We have to know this will be true for you
as it's true for all the ancients of the world—
the ones who've vanished into themselves,
the forgotten, the annoying, the silent,
the ones who sit vacant-eyed,
the ones who have forgotten how to cry.
We have to know this is true for us, too—
that you'll wait for us and greet us when we die.

You'll Hear the Sound

When winter comes around
you'll hear a silver-like musical sound
from the harbor whirling on shore;
that's Freddy Piercy dancing all around
letting you know he's still in town.
Listen softly; you'll hear the sound.

When winter comes around
you'll hear a spirited whooshing sound
from the pond where children skate;
that's Amy Iguchi spinning all around
letting you know she's still in town.
Listen sweetly; you'll hear the sound.

When winter crocuses rise above ground
you'll hear a lightsome laughing sound
near the train tracks on the south side of town;
that's Timmy Ryniker singing round after round,
letting you know he's still in town.
Listen tenderly; you'll hear the sound.

When spring comes around
you'll hear a gleeful violin-like sound
on the green in the park downtown;
that's Jonathan Purvis waltzing up and down
letting you know he's still in town.
Listen gently; you'll hear the sound.

Toward summer, you'll hear voices all around
from Main Street to Woodbine to Middleville Road,
from Waterside and down to the harbor in town;
that's Roberta and Eleanor and Timmy Lewis;
that's Joan and Sally and Jackie Posey
in a choir of angels who never saw twenty
letting you know they're still in town.
Listen joyously; you'll hear the sound.

George Harrison

What I hate is the way people say
George Harrison's in a better place;
so many places in this world
could have done as well—
if not Liverpool, then London;
if not London, then Delhi;
if not Delhi, then what about Rome?
We could have adorned his house with gold,
laid magic carpeting all across his floors,
hung pictures of sunshine on his every wall,
had flowers flown in from around the world.
And he could have stayed in that spruced-up place
writing songs and playing his guitar
for a good long weeping while.
It would have been that better place—
brighter, cheerier, less sprinkled with dust,
and not so far from us
and not so deep away
and not so darkening into rust.

Artist

When your mind went
so went your drawings
from sweeping pen strokes
to dull serrations—
the lurching and recoiling
of crayons in your fisted hand;
and you, frayed as the synapses
that groped for words
in your shrinking world.
When your drawings went
so went your voice
from full bass and rounded
to tinsel in wind;
and you, silenced
by the dumb recalcitrance
of senility and shine—
silver plate polished
to its hollow core.
So it was not suddenly
that you were no more.

For the Children

Here's the candle
and here's the flame
awakening darkness
as the river runs
down through woods
and grasses that whisper
all the way across the sea
where angels
dip their weary wings
to greet the children
who walk their way
along the lighted river path,
knowing God
is waiting on the other side.
Here's the candle
and here's the warmth
that lights their spirits
as they say goodbye
to Earth and family,
to sunrise and friends,
to rivers that run,
and the lighted candle
that melts in the sun.

My Old Dog, Juno

My old dog, where will you go
now your life is almost done?
I don't know if you know me now
or remember how you used to run
across the room for petting time,
across the lawn for chasing cats
and always to the kitchen at last
for a bowl of kibble and treats.

My old dog, where will you go
now that your life is almost done?
Will you think again of your time with me
and all our walks through parks and streets?
I don't know if you remember me now,
for our time together has been long, so long,
and you have passed from young to old
leaving me somewhere in between.

My old dog, where will you go
now that your life is almost done?
Will you still wake me in deep of night
and ask me to lift you up?
I don't know if you know who I am anymore,
but you seem to say you've been happy with me,
and we've spent these years watching evenings rise
along the road and into the yard.
And soon, I know, darkness will take you
far from me and into your grave.

Remember me, my old dog and friend.
And when I die, we'll sit side by side
watching the sun rise and evening fall,
and we will walk together again.

When You Loved Rick

When we were friends those years ago
we took our time sashaying through town,
flirting with boys and swinging our hair.
When we were friends we had no plan
to grow up or old or to dig for gold,
for life would work itself out in the end.
You loved Rick and I loved Charlie;
Rick loved the future and Charlie loved blondes;
you weren't the future and I wasn't blond,
so we went our four separate ways.
You moved uptown; I moved downtown;
Rick and Charlie married their darlings
who swung from rainbows and could pay the bills.
You and I weren't friends anymore,
and then we were, and then we weren't.
But we'd meet in midtown now and then,
you buying cigarettes, I walking the dogs,
and we'd look all around for things to say.
Too bad about Freddie and Karen and Carol;
looks like winter is here to stay.
How's your mother? And what about your sister?
Still living out in L.A.?
Nothing much new. Nothing much old.
Do you ever see Rick or Charlie in town?
Well, we'll have to have lunch
for old times' sake. How about
next April when spring comes around?

Mr. Biales, 1964

I really had a thing for Mr. Biales—
nothing about him was worldly or fine;
but he wore a black trench coat and said
I wrote like William Burroughs;
that's all it took to keep him on my mind.
He drove a 64 Chevy Cavalier
—a black box, brand new, and doomed—
and was saving his money for a trip
to New York, teaching night school
with adventure on his mind.
Behind his glasses and close-cropped hair,
I never knew who he was.
But he wore a black trench coat and said
I wrote like Henry Miller;
that's all it took to keep him on my mind.
I imagine he must have married
a girl with a bouffant and raised two kids
in the suburbs of Cleveland; and maybe
he was thinking I was seventeen and jailbait
and too far out for green lawns and narrows.
I really had a thing for that twenty-five-year-old—
nothing about him was glorious or sublime;
but he wore that black trench coat and said
I wrote like Allen Ginsberg;
that's all it took to make me love him;
that's all it took to keep him on my mind.

Being Ten: Missing Rebel

I miss my dog Rebel always at my side
on summer days as we tore across the beach.
I miss the hush of rain and the looping of tide,
our chasing after rainbows always out of reach.

On summer days when we tore across the beach
the breeze cooled our backs and swept out to sea;
we chased after rainbows always out of reach,
but we whooped with the power of running free.

The breeze cooled our backs and swept out to sea
and we kept on running until night rolled in,
but we whooped with the power of running free.
I miss the pounding of waves over the brim,

and we kept on running until night rolled in.
I miss George and his stories, his laughing eyes.
I miss the pounding of waves over the brim.
I miss Nancy and her ways of being wise.

I miss George and his stories, his laughing eyes,
and the howl of winter beyond the door.
I miss Nancy and her ways of being wise.
I miss Rebel's paws clicking across the floor.

I miss the howl of winter beyond the door,
seeping through windows and under the sheets.
I miss Rebel's paws clicking across the floor
I miss Rebel's smile, his warm breath and heat.

Seeping through windows and under the sheets,
the moon slipped through trees and slept on my bed.
I miss Rebel's smile, his warm breath and heat
even now after the years have left me for dead.

The moon slipped through trees and slept on my bed;
I miss moon shadows dancing up walls
even now after the years have left me for dead;
I think about my Rebel and running with the ball.

I miss moon shadows dancing up walls;
I miss Polly and pretending we were really wild horses;
I think about my Rebel and running with the ball.
I miss somersaulting across lawns and conquering such forces.

I miss Polly and pretending we were really wild horses
running over rocks and seaweed on the strand.
I miss somersaulting across lawns and conquering such forces,
and childhood and my dog and my long hair in a band.

Running over rocks and seaweed on the strand,
then sprawled on the ground counting stars at night,
and childhood and Rebel and my long hair in a band;
I miss sitting with my dog in golden moonlight.

Then sprawled on the ground counting stars at night
we could see all the way back to the beginning of time.
I miss sitting with my dog in golden moonlight
searching the star-glow for something sublime.

Stone On Stone: for Gloria

Yours is the most beautiful stone on South Drive;
a stone not like anyone else's,
a Stonehenge-like stone, only smaller, only lighter;
but still I wouldn't want to pick it up—
not only too heavy, it wouldn't be right;

although, and appropriately so, yours is the only plot
whose grass doesn't grow,
just like your old yard, unraked, untended,
but somehow more brilliant, more exuberant, yet mellow,
not like anyone else's.

I know you weren't really there, which is why I mentioned
as we continued talking,
"I know you're not really here."

The ink has already begun to fade on your dates,
on both opening and closing dates—like gates, of course,
in and out so quickly, despite its having taken so long—
you and your damned cigarettes.

I left a stone on your stone. It's tradition; it's a way
of connecting, of testing; like the princess and the pea—
if you can feel the weight of my tiny stone
on your Stonehenge of a stone, it means you know I was there,
and so you must have heard me telling you how pretty
and talented you were and how you would have enjoyed
today's sunshine and the shy flowers
just beginning to open their eyes
to whatever surprise lies in store before they close,
before tomorrow.

For the Love of Dogs

I have forgotten the names of so many heartbreaks,
forgotten their eyes, their lips, their smiles;
forgotten, even, why I loved them.
But I have never forgotten my sweet old dogs—

never forgotten my Rebel or Blackberry;
never forgotten my Geordie or Alec;
never forgotten my Scotty or Shane
or Chula or Juno,

never forgotten any dog—
not Ziggy or Jesse or Leo or Trixie or Sheba.

I have forgotten the names of so many heartbreaks—
old lovers who sailed out to sea;

and for a time I wished them back again;
I even cried; I plotted and planned
and wished they'd fly over the moon,
and wished they'd follow the pull of tide
and simple waves that licked the shoreline;
I tried to meet them on the roundabout road
or in a tunnel or far into night before the crack of any dawn;

but the sun one day turned purple to orange
and a new love sailed into bay
and whatever-his-name-was still sailed the sea
and I forgot to wish him back with me.

Not so my sweet dogs, not so my old dogs;
not so my Rebel or my Blackberry,
not so my Geordie or my Alec,
not so my Scotty, my Shane, my Chula, my Juno.

I have forgotten the names of so many heartbreaks;
but I have never forgotten the love of old dogs.

After Freedom, Home

Safe at home after fifteen minutes
over the fence and into the street,
Macgregor succumbed to his bath,
to the shampooing away
of whatever dead-ish, fecal-ish,
gum-sticking fetid matter
he had so joyously rolled in
during his sprint down the road.
Now subdued and still damp
from his bath, he smells of lavender
with hints of wet sweater,
and he seems content
to spend the night curled up
on the one dog bed he hasn't yet eaten.
Saki rolls his eyes at my indulgent
adoration of the prodigal son
whose tail wags even in sleep.

Walking Through Leaves

These trees won't notice when I don't walk here anymore;

they won't cry; they won't twist their arms across the sky,

won't look for my essence hidden by night or star

or fall of wind. They will sway as trees sway. They will grow

as trees grow—some straight into the sun, some twisting

around their own gray trunks, some bending forward as if

tracing shadows on the ground. They won't notice when I

don't come around anymore; they won't notice the trail

I've made walking here each day; won't notice when it's gone,

when it's obscured by snowfall, and leaves the road behind.

As though I never existed. As though my questions

about right and wrong and demands for justice, kindness,

and equality were as unsound and temporal

as the human species, as though the human species

never marked territory or ground, never made a sound.

Ann of Another Hour

Where did your mind go, my girlhood friend?
Is it napping in your blue coat pocket
or lost in the crumbling walls?
Pick up your childhood violin
and play a few bars of Bach or Ravel;
run your memory across the strings,
your fingertips along the neck.
Who is that woman who stole you away
and put on a gray-frown mask?
She's so much older than you ever were
and wears her hair pulled back,
her brow furrowed, her teeth yellowed,
and she bobbles in a sea of black.
Where did your sweetness go, my girlhood friend?
Did you tuck it under the grand piano
or under the bridge where the troll still lives?
Pick up a copy of Molière or Wilde,
and let's put on a comedy—
there'll be so much laughter and wiliness,
tip-toeing villains in ludicrous masks,
and cases of mistaken identity,
but everything will be well in the end.
We'll throw off our costumes and makeup then
and ride the old-time carousel
into the childhood of soft green hills.

For Ronnie Markman

I hear you changed your name to Brahmin
before you went into the desert,
that you filled your tent
with mint and rosemary,
with lavender climbing all in the door.
I hear you talked with spirit nymphs
who slid in on moonbeams at dawn of night,
who sang with you and played the sitar
while planting fields of pearl and starlight.
How many I've loved since loving you
and kissed in the wake of your memory
still tossing on the salt-brine froth;
how many times I've reached for you,
your blond hair blowing in the blue of time,
and you waving across centuries
to my single rose and gray of loss.

Questions

Where are ghosts
when we need them most?
Floating over the moon?
Perhaps sleeping in a vacuum
at the side of the road;
or are they waiting for us
on the cusp of life?

Where are old friends
who've left this earth?
Do they know we remember
the way they laughed?
Do they remember
the poems we read together?
Are they waiting for us
on the cusp of life?

Where is Rebel, my little dog,
who walked by my side
and slept beside me
when life fell cold?
Does he know my voice
after all these years?
Does he wait for me
on the cusp of life?

Where is Roy Rogers,
and his noble Trigger?
Are they riding across plains
in a movie reel? Do they
think of the children
who loved them in living
and wait for them
on the cusp of life?

And what about Cary Grant?
Is he a dapper angel
who can sing and dance?
Does he wander theaters
looking for his fans

or wait for them
on the cusp of life?

What of the people we would have loved
if their roads had merged with ours?
Are they starting life over
as princes or moonbeams?
Are they waiting their turn
on the cusp of life?

And what became of my mother?
Is she reciting Shakespeare
on a sky-blue stage
or living in her portrait
on the bedroom wall?
Does she wait for her children
on the cusp of life?

And what about me when I'm done
being me? Will I come back
as a frog or freeze like a rock?
Or will I wait in the dark
for a whisper of love?
Will I wait with angels
on the cusp of life?

Man to Window B

It's not easy to transform a grown man
into a window, especially a tall man,
a muscled man, and women swooning
over his eyes, his cerulean eyes,
over his touch, his feather touch;
especially a thinking man, a reading man,
a man who's been through storms and wars
and planted gardens;

but it happens all the time, beginning, always,
with a slow turn of the head, a hesitation
to go forward when the light turns green,
the girl in the car behind him giving him the finger;
proceeding to a confusion of words, a dropped word,
a runaway thought, a failure to finish the last sentence
or hear the doorbell's insistent blast;

and then meals picked at, neglected, forgetting
what a meal is for, the bursts of angry words
provoked by a shift in breeze or single floating
piece of dust; the wondering what that water thing is,
the thing in the you-know, in the room of the flushing;

and then dirt-crescent fingernails, white stubble on cheeks,
the raging and stamping through rooms;
the red thing with wheels in the yard that used to go places,
but has now forgotten how, the fire thing under the bubbling water—
not knowing how to make it stop,

and finally the fall, the ambulance, the screaming for help,
the *let me go, for Christ's sake let me go home*;
the white hair sparse and pasted against skeletal shoulders,
the gash on the sunken cheek, the rage, the threats,
the broken arm, the broken hip, the long corridors
of urine smells and flat pea-green.

And so the man is no longer a man—
he is Nurse Ginger's, Nurse Mike's;
he is Won't Eat; he is Can Get Violent,
Room 52, Window B.

To-Do List: Next Lifetime

Write more, don't care;
listen, hear, don't hear,
dump what doesn't matter.
Watch the signs, note the patterns,
say okay, walk away.
Take the words, ignore the words,
turn them around in your mind,
spit them out, pick them up,
write more, don't care.

Regard the eyes, not the color,
regard the glance, not the stare.
Watch for truths, watch for lies,
paint them yellow, paint them red,
turn them into pennies,
turn them into poems;
watch for signs, watch for patterns,
say okay, walk away.

Climb hills, not ladders;
swim at low tide, swim at high tide,
walk on water, fly over seas;
watch for truths, watch for lies,
draw them straight,
draw them spangled,
put them inside plated frames,
hang them all at crazy angles.
Write more, don't care;
observe what people
say and don't say.
Be you, not me; be free, be you.

Since Your Dying

You missed your birthday
you missed your dog crying
you missed the candle
you missed the flame
and wherever sun sets
you missed the golden
you missed the warning
of more to come;
you missed the rising
you missed the setting
and wherever arrows fall
you missed the mix-up
of good and bad;
you missed the loving
you missed the hating
you missed the sound of words
and wherever time stops
you missed the mourning
the wearing of black
the hours sobbing;
you missed the sunrise
you missed the starshine
inside the bandstand
when Louis played;
you missed his world
what a wonderful world
with trees of green
and red roses, too;
you missed the high notes
you missed the low notes
and wherever you are
you missed the eagles
wailing their wingsong
across the moon.

Dragonfly Lesson

You convinced me to go inside
rather than cut the grass today.

But given all the mosquitos and wasps
that have taken over the yard this year,

I shouldn't have assumed
you intended to nibble on me
or do me harm, but I did.

It was your bulging eyes, your dart body,
your expanse of wing, your ugly face
—there, I said it—

that made me think you were as brutal as a human,
as threatened and swift as a yellow jacket,
a predator on the attack.

I stayed in my room and googled your name.

Now it's dusk and grass still high,
mosquitos and wasps all but gone,
and thanks to you—

so tonight I'll meditate on concepts of beauty,
on wondrous eyes, and gossamer wings

that buzz when they beat, and lift,
and on you with your
full-circle vision, your mythical powers and fame—
bringing prosperity to China,
giving power to the Samurai,
outing little liars in Sweden.

Tomorrow I'll try again
in my long sleeves and knee-high boots
to cut the grass, to get along.

Perhaps Limbo

Sing kindness for the father
whose life winds down in chains
and rants; he used to say
death was a problem
more of disposal than of grieving,
but that was before the holding cell
between what was and what would come
filled with tears and spume.
Sing wisdom for the mother
never cited in history books
or rhyme; she used to say
life was a problem
to no one but the living,
but that was before the door locked
and she couldn't get out anymore.
Sing love for their children
who climbed to the peak of hills
and never went home again;
they used to say they'd stay forever;
like trees they swung and swayed,
but that was before the sun turned around
showing them the end of days.

Washing Clothes in El Salvador

My student says
she misses the days
when she used to beat
clothes on a rock
in the clear river
streaming through her village

in El Salvador
where everyone spoke
her language
without a struggle,
"My language,
it is more easier
than *inglez*," she says.

"Washing the clothes
in the rivers
is more nicer, too;
more better than the laundry-mat
where the lady,
she is mean to me
and she never laugh;
and my friends
they are not here
or the sunny days like there."

I tell her she should
write a poem about washing
clothes in El Salvador.
She smiles and glances
out the window where
the day is sunny and mild:
"The teacher, she so funny."

Cartoons

My father
drew cartoons
with swift
and simple lines
using pen and ink
on paper.

Sometimes
he would climb
into these lines
becoming
two dimensional
and so
very very comical,
and everyone
would laugh.

This is how
I remember him—
on paper,
and everyone
would laugh.

Christy In January

The end of January brings you back
in drifts of snow and cloud
as the thinning light of winter
deepens from pale to black;
and we hear again the winter song,
breaking twigs and cracking ice
on the pond where you once skated—
and then the possibilities and sighs
for what might or could have been.
How grown you would have been by now,
before your mirror wondering how age
would treat you in the end.
How the children you never had
would have grown by now
into young women and men,
the family gatherings and chinking of glasses,
the clock still chiming in grandfather's hall.
But none of this was, and all of this wasn't;
and we think of you softly, like snow,
at the end of each January when you come back
in the quiet of early dawn
when the light is orange and your breathing steady
and the empty pillow rises and falls.

Nancy's 100th Birthday

And we remember
when you would walk
in your high heels down
to the end of town
to buy a loaf of bread on sale,
and into stores
where you bought nothing
and then to home again
in your high heels
and faux-slit skirt
sewn by hand
those years ago.

And we remember
your parties bubbling
with champagne punch
and gold-specked damask;
and the full swing
of conversation
and clinking glasses
and Polonius's speeches
and the faux-jeweled glow
brushed crystal and rose.

And we remember how
you recited Shakespeare,
Shaw, and *Oh, to be in England
now that April's there*, and James
James Morrison Morrison
whose mother went down
to the end of town
and hadn't been heard of since.

And we remember your clear
blue eyes and the golden swing
of your waving hair
when you walked in your high heels
down-down to the end of town
to buy a loaf of bread on sale.

Thirty-Two Years
 (also for Nancy)

Windstorm shakes the mountain
in a brindle sky this evening
as lightning dives in daggers
across the gray-slope roofs;
and nothing tastes or feels of life,
nothing of hope in winter's song,
nothing of spring in early green—
just the hollow of hours in mourning.
You have passed beyond my reason
into the blink of candle's gleam,
a tremulous and dimming memory.
I pull the blanket over my head
and count the years flown by,
waiting in the dark for some sign from you
like laughter in rain or emerald eyes
winking from the moon.
Silent is the drummer boy
who walked by your coffin side;
silent also the daffodils
that grew along the garden fence;
and if music plays on the singsong wind,
it plays too low for me, and all around
the wide-flung trees, not a sound
or whisper from their leaves.

Returning

I have placed a candle in the quarry
should you return by way of rock.
I have planted seeds deep in the garden
should you return by way of rose.
I have emptied my heart into oceans
should you return by way of wave.
I have written your name in blackest clouds
should you return by way of rain.
I have whispered your poems in my sleep
should you return by way of dream.
I have folded a quilt in the cradle
should you return by way of child.
I have laid your memory in my grave
should you return by way of soul.

Letter to God

Let summer petals open in winter,
let felled redwoods rise again,
let crushed spirits bathe in sunshine.
And how about a world without murder?
You're God; you know how to do these things,
and what a whirl of a show you could give us.
Bring children back from death—
that's right—
unsnap their coffins and lift them up.
I've heard stories about that,
so I know you have the power do it.
Melt all the guns. Will you do that, too?
And don't tell me you've got your limitations,
because that's not what they teach
in prayer houses,
that's not what they teach
in good books,
that's not what the pilgrims say
on their way to Rome or Mecca or Shirdi.
Melt all the bombs while you're at it.
Melt hearts that pump only ice.
Melt mornings with disaster in store.
Melt all the bullets. Melt all the monsters.
Let poppies and irises push through snow.
Let yesterday's horror never have happened.
You're God; you know how to do these things.

End of Day

We packed your suitcase
with golden words;
we kissed you goodbye
and sent you on your way
beyond the spin
of this indigo world,
and a tolling of the bell
marked the end of day.

We kissed you goodbye
and sent you on your way
with a single wail
from the weeping wind,
and a tolling of the bell
marked the end of day,
but you held fast
to the white swan's wing.

With a single wail
from the weeping wind,
you had not a second
to turn back around,
but you held fast
to the white swan's wing
when night came forever
tumbling down.

You had not a second
to turn back around
when night came forever
tumbling down.
We packed your suitcase
with golden words,
and silver rained down
from the mountains.

First Rain, March 8

After a winter
that held on
like winter—
rain;

the scent of it
begins
uphill across
twin meadows

on the anniversary
of your dying,
settling
on keystrokes

of stories
still untold
or badly told,

of your time
that ended
too soon,

of books unwritten
since that winter
when you died
holding on
like winter
in the melting
of snow
into rivers—

the unforgiving
scent of it
resumes.

For Mr. G. Booth on His 86th

I wanted to send you a birthday cake,
but it didn't fit inside this poem;
so I thought perhaps a nice plate of beans,
but they shriveled up within the margins;
brownies—*well, sorry, I ate them*—cookies,
ice-cream, and every sort of fresh fruit pie
ducked and cowered in the smooth white spaces
between these lines—and nothing left to send.

So now the only thing to give you, George,
by way of a cordial birthday greeting,
are these strings of tidily printed words,
which are laid out here with candles in mind
and silver streamers strung across your years
and banners waving, and all the rivers
applauding you, and laughing cheering skies,
and starlight beaming from the mountain tops
reflecting all the good you've done and do.

Thank you for darling Mrs. Ritterhouse,
for the cross-eyed dogs with wobbly knees,
for twitching cats and single swung light bulbs,
for cluttered front yards and wacky front rooms,
for mechanics' gems and philosophies;
thank you for crisscrossing my path in life,
for being every inch of who you are.
Here's wishing you the happiest birthday
and all that's good and golden and God-kissed.

Old Merlin

I don't see why Merlin couldn't have been my father
or at least a beloved uncle;
he would have taught me the magic
of everyday tea leaves,
how to swoosh my baton in dead air
to make something like magic appear—
a garden without mosquitos, perhaps,
or a chocolate bar that never disappeared
no matter how much nibbling I did,
an A in algebra, and curly hair.

He would have been very bent and paper thin,
and everyone would have called him Grandfather,
but it wouldn't have mattered
because he would have been my first shining knight,
and for our nightly dinners everyone would have gathered
around the table with such laughter, honey wine, and bread.

He would have worn robes studded with star jewels,
sandals of hemp and hair to his shoulders;
and when he smiled his old-Merlin smile
his eyes would have lit all the candles in the city.
Elvis would have come to him for issues of style,
Pollack would have action-painted his constellation portrait,
Pavarotti would have married me just to be related to him,
and I would have lived in castles with high C's and pasta.

But Merlin was nowhere to be found
when I was hitchhiking on eternity's corner
waiting for my next father to stop his chariot
and carry me home. As it was, I was plucked up
by someone else, and things turned out the way they did.

November 22: The First Worst Day

Fifty years later; television
can't resist replaying
footage of the great fall,
the pink suit and afternoon
in Dallas with sunlight
bending across the barrel
of a rifle. News of it flew
in minutes around the world,
and all New York City
fell into silence—
trees poised in mid-sway,
birds, too, in mid-flight,
and shadows and dust
and cracks along walls
as we tried to will it a lie.
With blinking eyes
we looked at the sky
as though it had answers
or meaning or light,
as though it could convince
death to snatch a different,
less God-stung life.

The day after his election,
Carol Larsen told everyone
in social studies class,
This is going to be one sorry country.
She was right, but not
because her man didn't win
(although he did some time later,
and we became even sorrier).

That weekend we learned
how special we were not,
how God was not on our side,
after all. We re-read Camelot
and re-read Camelot
and found that time and fire
don't care how beautiful your dress,
how perfect your mind,

your body, your bank account—
we are dung beetles and fleas to time;
we are the fire's kindling,
ashes to ashes for one and all.

We climbed into our apartments,
tuned in to Walter Cronkite,
saw him take off his glasses
and choke back sobs, saw him
take off his glasses and swallow
his sorrow as though it were a toad
that would eat him alive.
The clock behind him
in the TV studio still ticked
as clocks once did, still jerked
from minute to minute as we clung
to the last sparkle of sinking dusk,
trying to turn back the tide, the sorrow,
searching for some reason
to embrace our tomorrows.

Full Flower Moon for Nick, Vicky, Alan, & Greg

No one is talking about it—
not in public;

they don't want copycats
to follow your lead,

so they try not to make
a big deal of it—

no assembly, no memorial,
no photographs in the halls;

just a brief announcement
and moment of silence.

Notice how I haven't revealed
what you did

or how you did it;
notice how I haven't lectured you

about tomorrow's sunlight
or rosebuds among thorns.

Notice how I haven't expressed
any anger, how I labor

to lay my words softly,
to sound understanding;

because I do understand
that it all seemed insufferable,

too much and dragging you down,
too many twisters and hailstorms

for someone so young
and tender as you.

Notice how I haven't said

who you were or could have been

or pointed to green hills
you might have climbed

or shown you pictures of countries
or gardens or seasides

or mentioned what wonders
you could have seen.

Notice how I haven't said anything
about last night's full moon

or told you that some Native Americans
would call it the Full Crow Moon

because it appears with the caw of the crow
to announce the end of wintertime.

Notice how I haven't mentioned
that winter is followed by spring,

which swings on the face
of the Full Fish Moon

as fish swim upstream to spawn,
as May paints its chorus of colors

under the light
of the Full Flower Moon.

Kofi Awoonor

Where have you gone,
Kofi Awoonor?
Are you sitting with Ghandi
over tea and angels?
Perhaps reborn as star
or wildflower,
or parading as winter
in a far-off land.
And what of the poets
of Ghana?
And what of the poets
of Earth?
Are we all to be murdered
by ignorant fools
whose guns are mightier
than love or word?

The Baron's Restaurant on the Danube

Perhaps it was wicked of us to show up
that night at your restaurant on the Danube
with our smiles and glances and memories.
But we wanted to see how you were doing;
we wanted to see how you fared
after so many years of not speaking.
Strange that you didn't notice us waving
when you returned to the restaurant from hunting;
a pity you left the room so quickly
instead of coming over to say hello
or asking if we were enjoying our meal.
Perhaps you had to get busy skinning your kill;
perhaps you were wanted
in the wine cellar or kitchen.
Well, never mind, there's always next time.
I'd like to compliment you
on the sumptuous menu and elegant
presentation of platters and plates.
Of course, we didn't eat the small animals
you brought in on the barrel of your gun,
and we stayed away from the butter and cream,
because, as you may not have noticed,
we've kept ourselves trim.
The spinach pie was just moist enough
and the salad so pleasingly cut,
the bread, too, with its delicate crust.
And I mustn't neglect the décor—
so spacious, yet cozy and softly lit,
so rustic, yet classic, with paintings
of hunters carrying dead ducks
and trudging, at dusk, from the forest.
Well done, dear Baron, you've created a marvel;
it's almost as though you had no past,
no memory of strife or friendship or love;
it's almost as though you've always been Baron—
Baron of the Danube and the easy life.

Fifty Years of Cultural History

The lean and Dylan years were the bomb; everyone dragged
around smoking grass, tobacco, and even aspirin, and no one gave a
damn. Our favorite expressions were *out-a-sight* and *far out*; our names
were *Man* or *Rainbow*; our questions—*S'up*? *What's goin' down*? And
when we got really profound, we'd say *dig* or *far out* or *yeah*.

Camelot had lasted 1036 days; then the Beatles came in with smiles,
wanting to hold our hands. There was war undeclared, yet people still
died; there were bombs, napalm, and families slaughtered, because that is
war, is war, is war.

There were parties and diamonds on the White House lawn; Sinatra and
Sammy Davis shifted sides. Then the war was over and nothing left to
protest but the pudgy and Nixon years; everyone learned to believe in
make-believe, and Joan Baez sort of disappeared; but we were happy to
have George Carlin and the Smothers brothers on our side, and we
laughed sharply on blades of knives.

Dylan got himself whooped up and electrified—his voice amped like a
big bassoon; Judy Collins sang with the Muppets; and having a gun and
shooting *whatever* up became a matter of personal pride; blood ran thick
down alleyways, old hippies grew bald spots and fat. Genuflecting to the
trendiest of drugs, everyone dressed in pin stripes and glitter and
bounced from club to club.

Andy Warhol died for no reason at all, Jim Fixx, Jim Henson, Jimmy
Hendrix, and Janice. Presidents came and went—one got shot and
invented trickledown; music got louder and people got fatter; women
wanted a voice and got it; and, just to say they were sorry for getting it,
they called one another *guys*.

People bought guns and killed at will and got to be heroes on the news
that night. John Lennon was murdered in icy cold blood, and Yoko Ono
got respect at last. Gentle George Harrison got sick and died, and
everyone played "My Sweet Lord" for a year and cried.

Music got louder, the louder the better; rich kids shot up and died; music
got meaner, the meaner the better, poor kids shot up and died. Stupid was
smart, televisions ruled, and Dylan gave credit to the Muse; and Dylan
gave credit to the Muse.

Now everything Elvis ever sang is a classic, and Facebook is where we meet our friends; Pavarotti is gone; so is Hop-A-Long, Roy Rogers, and Allen Ginsberg; McCartney and Jagger dye their hair brown; beauty is industry, big lips are in, and faces don't move in anger or pain; the Dalai Lama still has no home, and Dolly Parton still goes on tour. Everyone says the economy is tanking, but there's always money for facelifts and war.

Dear Orchid

The directions said
to place three ice cubes
on the soil under your leaves
once a week,
to keep you
in a bright room
but not in direct sunlight.
I have done all that
and even sung to you;
yet, your petals lie curled
and dying on the counter top.
What have I missed?
In what way amiss?
Alas, it's not
that I didn't love you enough
or appreciate
your pink and delicate
scent.
True, I've been busy
—some say distracted—
but there was praise,
there were glances,
violins and sweetness
in the air.
The directions said
no one could kill you,
not even if they tried,
and I swear to you
I didn't even try.
Three ice cubes. Check.
Bright room. Check.
No direct sun. Check.
What have I missed?
In what way amiss?

Eleanor Jones, 1826
(for my great great great grandmother)

Young woman gives birth
at Chepstow Workhouse.
They say it's a boy, thank God for that;
he won't end up like the mother—
what was she thinking?
did she think he loved her?

did she think she was special?
did she think he'd stay?

another conquest for Squire Lewis;
another newborn without a father;

what was she thinking when he
lifted her skirt?
did she think he'd give over his name?
did she believe in fairytales and forever more?

They say it's a boy, thank God for that,
he won't end up like the mother—
what was she thinking after scrubbing his floors,
after curtseying at the door,
after saying good night?

did she think he would walk with her
or give her his arm—
his arm, his glance, his gentleman's silks?
did she think he would invite her
to breakfast next morning?

They say it's a boy, thank God for that,
he won't end up like the mother—
another house maid sent packing in heart-sob
from Lewis Manor to Chepstow's door.

Giving Thanks

For questions
impossible to answer,
for midnight's pearl
of starshine,
for Carl Sagan
who unveiled the cosmos,
for illness
that brings understanding,
for understanding
that brings laughter,
for the great comedy
of growing old,
for narrow roads
that lead to the piazza,
for wide roads
that disappear into oceans,
for the mother I had
who didn't mind questions,
for the friends I've had
who weren't really friends,
for the friends I have
who were and are,
for dogs who wag their tails
and know all the answers,
for mornings
whose promises aren't yet broken,
for broken promises
that gave me back my freedom,
for places to be before I go
to places I haven't yet been.

4:10 A.M.

It's dark and morning shivers;
throwing aside the bedcovers
becomes a declaration

irrational is rational,
a signing of the warrant for my
own arrest;

curious how willingly I drag myself
out of bed and pick up
the gauntlet
of another dawn.

St. Gabriel's Park, NYC

You were the garden
that led me and followed,
the shadow that waved
on late afternoons
even when the sun
hid behind buildings
on the avenue where
we were born and died,
where traffic never stopped
and footsteps plodded
toward the path in the park
where grass never grew.
Up through seasons,
snowfall, and flooding,
up through the river
on the east side of town
where tugboats sounded
their proud morning mission
and school unbolted its doors
on Thirty-Third and Second,
where we ran shouting
into high noon and whispers,
racing to the end
of woven steel fences,
climbed to the top,
and never looked down.

Christy

In the photograph, you're holding
my daughter on your lap.
My other two daughters flank you,
and their friend sits beside
your contemplative sister.
You are dark-eyed and thoughtful,
for you are the oldest in this tribe
and take seriously your role
as big sister and friend.
When I looked through the lens
I had no way of knowing
the world would lose you so soon;
when I looked through the lens,
I saw only an instant,
captured you there for 1000 eons.
Had I known, I would have taken
a million photos, reminding you
with each click how lovely you were.
I would have told you to run past moonlight
across fields and roses and never look back.
Had I known, I would have given you
a ticket to green lands and built you
a staircase to cross any rainbow.
But you had nothing of that from me;
you had your own road to run,
your own way back. Had I known,
I would have told you how beautiful
you were and written your name
in the heart of my poems, and wished
your lifetime into hours of peace.

No, Pete Seeger, They Will Never Learn

Oh, great, another war. Let us go to war
and just to make it seem okay,
let's call it duty, honor, patriotism;
and let's label coward, communist,
and traitor anyone who disagrees.

Oh, great, another war. Let us go to war
and let's create enemies where none
existed before, and let's call them
terrorists, extremists, and baby killers
and kill anyone who disagrees.

Oh, great, another war. Let us go to war
and let's make the people pay
for our weapons and propaganda;
let them buy our ammunition,
let them bury their soon-to-be dead
with all sorts of pomp and circumstance,
with marches, flags, and taps.

Oh, great, another war. Let us go to war
and let's not use the word *war*;
let's call it conflict or intervention;
let's call it the triumph of freedom.
Let's drop bombs; let's kill people
and animals and destroy the land;
and, just to be safe, we'll call these things
unfortunate collateral damage and repeat words
such as *hero*, *flag*, and *sacrificial*.

Oh, great, another war. Let us go to war
and let's pretend that war is noble,
that God wants us, not them, to win.
And when our enemies, friends, and relatives
are blown to pieces and gathered in graves,

let's lay flowers at their simple headstones,
let's pray for peace across the world
while mercenaries count their winnings,
while gun makers take new orders
from politico-villains who hide their earnings,
and the winds of revenge are born again.
And they will never learn, Pete Seeger;
and, no, they will never learn.

Forgotten

What difference if you've forgotten
the moon,

its glow that night over the Arno
silver enough

to pull us from sleep;

what difference if you've forgotten
Fiesole,

its colors still mixed by Fra Angelico's brushes,
or the amphitheater still applauding

Dionysius pirouetting on stage;

what difference if you've forgotten
the meteor shower

raining emerald that night
through purple-dark skies

washing us into the sea;

what difference if you've forgotten
my name

by now, by yesterday, or tomorrow's
moon-drench

stippled in the salt of remembering.

This Is What I've Done
(for my daughters)

I have left for you
a bowl of apples
to bake into a pie,
a tree of lemons
for the end of springtime
to plant into a grove.
I have brushed each moonrise
along the skyline,
painted these high walls
in perfume of lime,
sung these low notes
in emerald of valley,
swung across the trapeze sky
in diamond-glow of dawning.
And when you remember,
as I know you will,
you'll notice me swinging
on a sun-struck raindrop
on the crest of the green-briar hill,
and I'll be writing
your names in stardust;
I'll be applauding your songs.

www.ingramcontent.com/pod-product-compliance
Lightning Source LLC
Chambersburg PA
CBHW060702030426
42337CB00017B/2720